In Orbit, Back Soon

David Viney is a multiple [illegible] slam winner, playwright, workshop facilitator and [illegible] Stretford, Gtr Manchester. He has bee[illegible] [illegible]alling festival, written for and [illegible] performed two shows [illegible] Working Verse Collect[illegible] write and perform at th[illegible] the World Taekwondo Champions[illegible] s his second solo poetry collection.

To Diane,
Thanks for the support,
All the best,
Dave Viney

By the author

A Poet Called Dave
In Orbit, Back Soon

Praise for *A Poet Called Dave*

"Poignancy without pretension, scalpel sharp insight. Viney's observations on class and culture are deft, powerful and bull's-eye accurate."
Byron Vincent, poet & playwright

"One of the authentic voices of Manchester. Can be funny, sincere and compassionate in one fell swoop."
Dr Jo Bell, former Director National Poetry Day

"An extremely talented poet, both on stage and the page."
Marvin Cheeseman, poet

"Funny, incisive, poignant."
Jonny Fluffypunk, poet & playwright

"A very funny man and ten times more talented than he is funny."
Mike Garry, poet

"At first I thought he was going to try and steal my handbag, but instead he stole our hearts! And my handbag."
Thick Richard, poet

★★★★★
Goodreads

DAVID VINEY

IN ORBIT, BACK SOON

Flapjack Press
flapjackpress.co.uk

Exploring the synergy between performance and the page

Published in 2021 by Flapjack Press
Salford, Gtr Manchester
flapjackpress.co.uk Flapjack Press
FlapjackPress Flapjack Press

ISBN 978-1-8384703-0-2

daveviney.co.uk
vineypoet vineypoet

Artwork, illustrations & photos courtesy of the author

Cover photo by Sajjad Ahmadi
Courtesy of Unsplash

Printed by Imprint Digital
Exeter, Devon
digital.imprint.co.uk

FSC

MAN CHE STER
A UNESCO City of Literature

Contents

This is going to seem like a strange way to introduce poetry, but bear with me...

Between the ages of fourteen and sixteen, I racked up nine police cautions. They were all for petty crimes (although I suppose how petty they really were depends on the people they affected). I was the younger idiot mascot for a larger, older group of idiots. Most of those cautions were a mix of boredom, mis-adventure and dumb luck. Some were peer pressure. Some were sheer stupidity. None were violent or the work of a criminal mastermind. By the fifth or sixth I knew most of the officers at Stretford Police Station by name. They saw through the act: I was cheeky but funny; foolish but not vicious. And undeniably shit at being a criminal. Although to be fair to my criminal *potential*, a lot of the things I got in trouble for were nothing to do with me – I just had the shortest legs in a chase. Even some of the things that *were* me, weren't me; I'm not saying I'm Oliver Twist, but older lads forcing younger lads to steal has been around since Day Dot. I was a kid out of his depth, sinking in plain sight of the law and they begrudgingly liked me. Under the circumstances we became overfamiliar.

Being around violence had become so normal that if you'd told me at the time there were fifteen-year-olds who'd never been hit, I would've laughed in your face. If you'd told me that some people go through their *entire lives* without ever experiencing physical violence, my head would have exploded.

To elaborate (in a way that every kid who grew up in similar circumstances will instantly recognise), sporting equipment can take on a sinister alter-ego when used out of context. When I see a baseball bat, my first thought is definitely not baseball. It's a wincing flashback of a kid called Stephen trying to use my head for a home run and thankfully only catching my shoulder. Same goes for golf clubs (broken nose), cricket bats (chased down the street), hockey sticks (friend mistaken for a puck) – once you've been hit by them, they stop representing sporting excellence. And if we think we had it bad, spare a thought for Russian kids… a report by Russian news agency TASS says Russians purchased over 500,000 baseball bats in one year, but only one recorded purchase of a baseball.

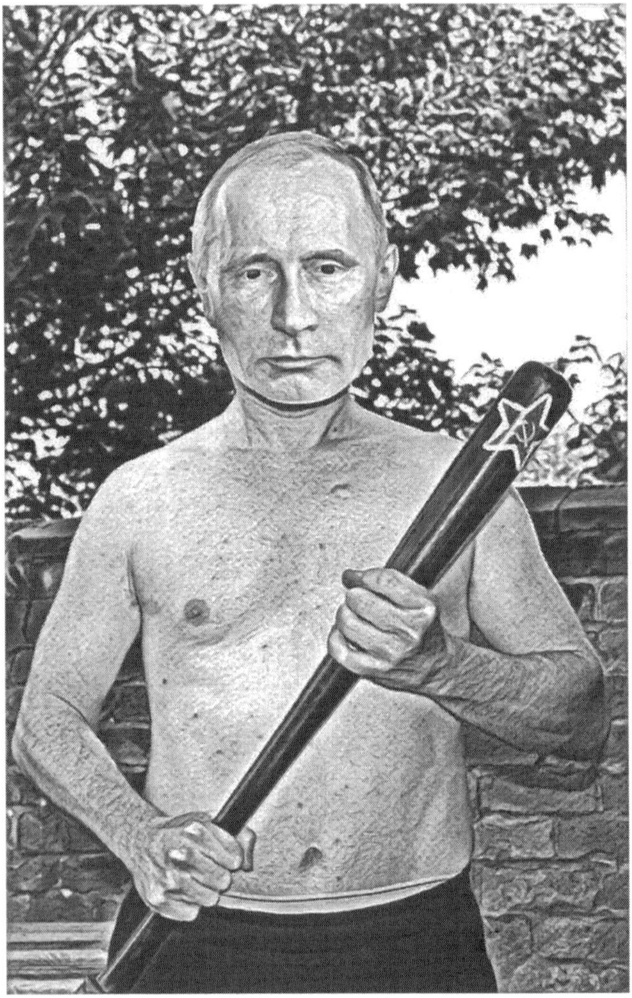

We'd moved about a bit by the time we landed in Trafford and I'd experienced plenty of hostility along the way. But it didn't prepare me for the brutal pantomime I would witness on the streets and parks of Stretford in my teens. It was not uncommon to see lads in their mid to late teens / early twenties approach others of a similar age, strangers, and strike up friendly conversation before launching a physical onslaught mid-sentence that they had no time to defend. If they had anything of value, they were robbed (or 'taxed' as it was commonly referred to back then) and I sensed a twisted pride in their ability to gain their victim's trust, before catching them off-guard.

It didn't take me long to work out that I wasn't like that. But it took a lot longer to distance myself from it. There's a general misconception that *Home* automatically equals safety. We were a one-parent household. Mum, as tough as she was, is five foot three. When two lads (who you've seen perpetrate horrendous acts of violence) knock on your door and ask your mum politely if you're in, before telling you once she's out of earshot that if you don't come out they'll punch her in the face, your options instantly reduce to one.

And so I was always out. I became skilled at avoidance and blagging my way out of corners. I developed a knack of wisecracking humourless hard cases and catching a beating for it at a later date.

This situation had not gone unnoticed by my unlikely chums at Stretford Police Station, who were now bestowing worldly wisdom with every Caution. The tone remained awkwardly upbeat. But we all knew that if our paths kept crossing, it was only a matter of time before they'd be forced to charge me with something.

Their masterstroke came in the form of an ambush; I would always make sure they called dad to pick me up. He didn't live with us and though I knew he'd be angry, mum had a certain unpredictability when it came to a bollocking that was never physical, but somehow made me more nervous of her reaction.

This time, as I left, they told me I had to report back to the station in a week. They knew I'd consider not going and then remember they knew where I lived, so a week later I sloped in brimming with cheek and ready to break out the funnies. Straight away I knew something was up. They were less chatty and more officious; smiles replaced with tight-lipped sternness. The cop who escorted me deeper into the station than I'd ever been before said only one word, "Behave", so when we stopped outside Inspector Shorrock's office all cockiness drained away; *this is where he congratulates me on beating the record for Cautions and hands me my winning ticket to Youth Offenders*, I thought.

That door opened in instalments, every increment revealing a thin slice of room that I dreaded entering and then, to my absolute horror, I saw mum.

What followed was the best use of a prop I've ever seen – mum sat in a chair, never spoke, barely moved – as Shorrock spoke of her embarrassment, of her selfless struggle as a single mum of two, of my apparent lack of respect for her… He struck every chord I'd muted and he made the Desk Sergeant's well-meaning advice seem fortune cookie by comparison. I remember shame kicking over chairs inside me and a real sense that I'd just witnessed the power of words.

And in case you're wondering, mum had plenty to say when we got home.

It took more than a talk. And Shorrock may well have rolled that shtick out to every kid he spoke to. The point is not that he's Ghandi (he could be an absolute arsetrumpet for all I know). The point is that his talk / those words, left an indelible imprint on me. It took a couple of years of spending as much time in other places as I could, of making real friends, of being in the orbit of girls, of laughing without worrying it would be taken the wrong way and lead to a fight, then with more years came the gradual disbanding of Stretford gangs by age, by prison sentence, by life.

I was lucky then and I've been lucky enough to work with

young offenders since. I started telling this story as an example of the life-changing possibility of words. If you're reading this, chances are you're already a closet, or *fully out* Word Nerd, so I'll just say that words changed the course of my life for the better. I've made my apologies – I realise that in my case the shadow of the loveable rogue bears an uncanny resemblance to the shadow of the little shit. Maybe I was somewhere in the middle – the notsobad nob'ead? All I know for certain is that if you do find yourself in possession of a way with words and in a position to positively affect the life of a young person, you should definitely look beyond the labels (*trouble / bad kid*) and the limiting timescales (*past saving / had their chance*) to the variables and the backstory.

Here we are…

A second poetry book and over a decade attempting to craft words into a meaningful connection with other human beings. It's been a massive waste of everybody's time.*

You may have noticed and be wondering why this second book is 'David' Viney and not 'Dave'. The answer (well, the main reason) is that my mum has always hated me calling myself Dave and always called me David – I've finally relented, mum. But to be honest, as names go, 'Dave' is not received particularly well in poetry circles. I touched on it jokingly in the first book. It was supposed to be a statement of defiance; a preconception to burst out of like a giant birthday cake. But I've made my peace with preconception – it ain't going anywhere – and the stage and page are still the best places to set people straight.

* Only kidding, it's been ace (for me at least). I've had a blast.

I'm not complaining – it hasn't stopped me doing most of the things I set out to do. I've performed at a lot of brilliant nights, at festivals, on stage at the Manchester Arena live on TV, in squats, with bands, performed plays at the Lowry Theatre and the Edinburgh Fringe, hosted poetry nights and events, won some poetry slams, lost plenty of poetry slams, written and facilitated workshops with Arts Organisations and great charities like Amnesty International, Headspace and Mancspirit, had an absolute *artcrush* of mine (Maxine Peake) do a video to one of my poems, recorded a track for a charity album that also features Johnny Frickin Marr, written two books – I've been busy – so if the name Dave is, or has been an issue for you at any point, please feel free to send me a list of better, more worthy names and I'll send you a list of what you can do with them.

A lot of people call me Viney as a default anyway and I already use David for plays and TV / film script work (I wasn't making that mistake twice you picky fuckers ☺). Not sure I'm fully retiring 'Dave' yet though – I do worry that if I do, I'll wake up the next day and find I have a wardrobe full of sensible jumpers.

I could always just use the name VINEY, like MORRISSEY. Yeah, maybe not.

One big Davey Bonus has been cabaret nights – they love a good Dave don't they. They probably initially think they're getting a crude, working class male version of Pam Ayres and touch wood, so far they've been pleasantly surprised when I instead turn out to be a crude, working class version of me.

For the *Preconcepticons* – that's a joke!

I *am* a big advocate of performing at cabaret nights though – they flex different muscles, force you to win crowds that are never fully yours. You have to share them with the band, the comedian, the singer-songwriter, the burlesque dancer… it keeps you on your toes and sharpens your audience interaction. Gigs like Shangri La in Prestwich and Tickle Your Fancy (in Chorlton and various other towns and cities) feel like home and the masochist in me likes the challenge of winning over a *non-poetry* crowd. To be honest, after 2020/21 and such limited stage time, I'm hoping we get creative and have more variation in performance spaces – the world's a stage is probably the truest of the dead metaphors. Gig in your garden? Yeah, why not. Gig in a carpark? Sign me up. Gig in your bathroom? Logistical nightmare mate. Put some clothes on and let's never speak of this again.

If you're buying this book from a book shop or online, thank you, and although the physically distanced nature of your purchase is in keeping with the horrible shitshow that has blighted 2020/21, please consider this book a HUG TOKEN with no expiry date, redeemable if we ever meet in person.*

If you're buying this book at a gig and such things are allowed, COME HERE YOU!

* Terms and Conditions apply: The Hugg(er) reserves the right to reject the Hugg(ee) under any of the following circumstances: worldwide pandemic, unidentifiable smell, persons currently or previously nicknamed 'Crusher' or 'Spine-cracker', soap-baddy eyes, kidnap plot, pick-pocket, plagiarism, the pong of opulence, arrest warrant.

Welcome

Welcome to Viney's Value Vernacular

This book is self-service.
Please choose from the following options:

- My thoughts
  poured out like cold alphabet soup
  onto paper plates.
- My thoughts
  warmed by the imaginary recital
  of Sean Connery
  (or a silky-tongued orator of your choosing).
- My thoughts
  Free from artificial additives.
- My thoughts
  spilled like milk and tears.
- My thoughts
  (may contain traces of nuts).

Welcome Home

Home.
Dawn.
The transient glow of the night before.
The windows tint.
The wood breathes easy.
The letterbox yawns
and the hinges whisper.
The roof tiles sigh
under the calming caress
of a sympathetic sun.

Home.
Mid-morning.
Fortified flophouse.
Comedown castaway.
The blinds sharpen and prepare to repel.
The letterbox clenches its jaw.
The gutters ready boiling drudge.
The wood rubberizes to absorb knuckles.
The Welcome Mat amends its message
in a most impolite manner.

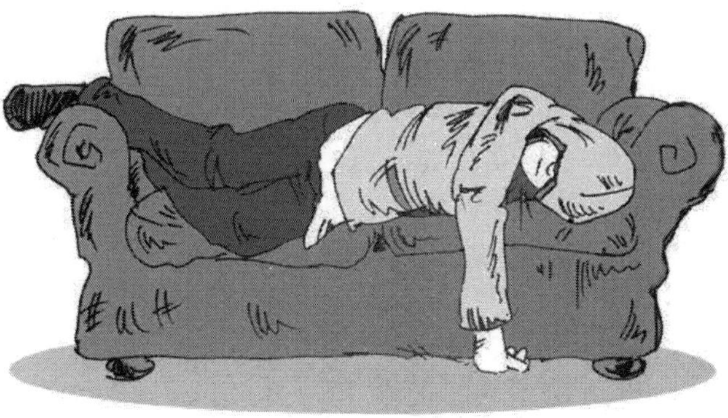

Welcome to the Terror Globe

A poem on the off-chance that extra-terrestrials exist.

Welcome to the Terror Globe,
where conflict as a capitalist construct is not even news
and cage rattling is a national sport.
Where historical lessons are doubtcast, undermined
and publicly untaught.
Where the fair fight is a knuckle duster
in a boxing glove
and the public's mental health is a bloodied, toothless grin.
Where Presidents remote-detonate activism to their own ends
and peace is just the pause before the axe swings.

Welcome to the Terror Globe,
where your heart can be a candy-filled piñata
or a rotting corpse-filled skip.
Either one is fine.
Where the truth's on the tip of tongues
trapped behind stitched lips.
But there's an effluent flow of lies.
Where beards are seen as sinister
on the face of the Middle Eastern.
But you can kill with clean-cut impunity
if you become an American policeman.

Welcome to the Terror Globe,
where the tense thriller you were promised
is actually a horror triple-bill.
A sneak peek behind the green screen
reveals a writhing mass of wretched, screaming egos
and the popcorn tastes like roadkill.

Welcome to the Terror Globe,
where anxiety is applied like pepper-spray
and acceptance live-streamed from the treadmill.
Where good luck is a falling piano
and bad luck a falling orchestra.
(If the cellist doesn't get you, the bassoon player will.)

Welcome to the Terror Globe.

You're welcome to the Terror Globe.

Welcome to Adventureland

Welcome to Adventureland,
where adventure can land you in the back of a police van.
Where the man-size Tonka Truck rides have to be hot-wired
and the slippery slope of bad ideas
is vandal-greased for extra speed.

Welcome to Adventureland,
where the entrances are side fence, back fence
and *off*ence.
Legitimate entry strictly prohibited.
It's where likely lads can form a queue
for razor-wire epiphanies.

And you won't find it in your wardrobe.
Don't go climbing any beanstalks.
Adventureland cannot be found
in the Enchanted Forest you speak of.

It's the tumble-guts of future homes
that we can only dream of –
where shady mates play Shakes & Ladders,
a loaded dice gets rolled…
and you find yourself 40 feet up and still climbing
the largest ladder of all…

The **what were you even thinking?!** crane.

And it's hands down
the most responsibility yours have ever had.
The baddest of bad decisions.
Although perfectly in line with
Adventureland's Terms & Conditions.

No health and safety.
No compensation.
Adventureland could not care less about your social situation.
It's next level hazardous.
Revels in the perilous.
A Mecca for forgettable expendable adventurers…

because when you pass 100 feet straight up
you have a serious word with yourself.

When you pass 200 feet
you start to question the mechanics of hands –
their ability to cling to life
and a crane that reaches into the night sky
like Zeus's arm, fist clenched around a bolt of lightning.
But the only gods you've ever known
have made it very clear that they don't like you,
so you put your junk-mail hopes
and your straight to voicemail prayers
into the fingers you have no faith in
and you climb
and you climb
and you climb
and you climb
until you see a portrait of a dark, moody
cloud-infused sky
or a portal to the stars –
as alien as the picture-perfect families
you imagine inhabiting the half-built homes below
and you emerge through that hatch to the top platform
a changed man – birthed by bravado.

SPOILER ALERT!!

The view from the top platform is good.
But after that, all that's left
is the unbearably normal,
magically bereft,
impossibly small,
nothing like the hype at all
Driver's Cab

(which is of course locked
in case some idiot climbs 265 feet
to see if it's open).

It consists of a battered leather seat
(complete with builder's bum imprint),
a discarded crisp packet (faded),
and some important-looking levers and buttons.
All secure behind a muppet-proof door.
That's what you've won.

And when the reverse nightmare of down is done,
at the end of your daredevil display,
Adventureland will not honour you
with a tickertape parade.
No banners will hail you a hero.
No brass band will play.
You will be bathed in the blue light of 'justice' my son;
baptised in the tears of distraught mothers
who couldn't find the words to explain
that those childhood stories of adventurous youths
who never took the blame,
were dependent on where those youths came from
and the value attached to their name.

DANGER
CONSTRUCT ON SITE
KEEP OUT

WELCOME
ON THEN
GET ON
WitH
IT

Weekend

Short term memory loss…
As sober as a judge
with a crack habit.
Shot glass goddess.
Pint pot prodigy.
The line that wrote
'In orbit, back soon'
across your face.
The pill that swallowed time
and you whole.

The Circus of Weekend.

Step right up folks…
see the incredible
jaw-jiving, space-invading,
saucer-eyed Lol Monkeys
waterboard the inner voices
that tell us we're a carpet burn
on the arse of the world.

Marvel
as Mollie walks the *high-wired*
with no safety net and one shoe.
Witness Mancunian astronaut Mason
get the rocket from his girlfriend.
Not the first spacedman to moon
on Planet Spangled,
where gravity is a prankster.

One small step for man,
one giant leap for man-caned.

Don't Try This at Home

Is that leather?
It looks like leather.
It can't be leather.
We can't afford leather.
It had better not be leather.
Whether it's leather or not is irrelevant now,
because in quarter of an hour mum gets home
and we're gonna *get* leathered!

Little brother's wearing a thousand-yard stare,
dwarfed by mum's favourite armchair.
Pale like Skeletor pales in comparison
to mum when she's on one.

That's the problem with dares…

It never ends there.
Single dare becomes double dare.
Double dare becomes triple dare.
And then before you know it…

"Quadruple dare!! It means I dare you times four."
"Yeah, well I quin…I quint…"
"Ah, you don't know!"
"Neither do you, idiot! Anyway, I dare you more!"

That was four thirty.
Fast forward to twenty to five
and I have transformed
from 12-year-old Mancunian muppet Dave Viney
into 12-year-old Mancunian mercenary Dave Rambo;

tea-towel tied around my head
and instead of an M60 high-calibre machine gun
I've got a kitchen knife.
They're easier to come by.

And I'm brandishing it.
You can't just *hold* one in your hand.
I know this, because I read it in the paper.

And I'm standing five feet or so away
from my younger brother,
who could be better,
in a chair, that could be leather –
telling him,
"Don't worry about it.
This is a classic knife-throwing stance.
I saw it in a film."

Feet shoulder width apart,
arm folded at the elbow,
blade gripped between thumb and forefinger.
"Now remember,
don't flinch."
Listen,
I have no intention of throwing this knife at him.
But I'm his older brother –
If I don't make him fear for his life, then who will?

Through the wall to next door
we hear a low rumble.
He hears next door's tumble dryer.
I hear a drum roll…

Arm arcs downwards double speed.

Me – sweat on.
Him – spot on impersonation of Deirdre Barlow
during a particularly intense row with Ken,
all bulging eyeballs and neck veins and then
the unthinkable happens:
the blade slips out of my grip,
too quick for quick thinking.
Blink and you'll miss him flinching
and me closing my eyes,
saying my first prayer since primary school…

Eyes screwed tight.
Unscrew left.
Unscrew right.
No knife at first sight.
Health check:
- Face – traumatised
- Neck – neck
- Shoulders – rigid
- Arms – twitching
- Torso – torso
- Legs – disco
- Overall Prognosis – therapy

So where is he hiding this knife?

Little brother stands,
legs *Bambi*fied.

Walks four feet as faun,
leans on a wall
and lets out a loud non-punctured lungful
of *WTF*.
That's 'What The Flip' – he's only seven.

His lust for life is just beginning
but I know my life is finished;
mum gets home in ten minutes
and though neither of us wants to admit it,
there is definitely a kitchen knife
sticking out of her favourite chair.

I beg the clock to stop ticking.
But it's just a clock.
I beg the sun to stay out.
But it's getting dark.
I have one plan:
run away and live in the park.

Little brother's not listening –
he's still in shock.
I hear a key being turned in the front door lock…

The Interview

They say the closest you'll ever come to perfection
is when you fill out a job application form,
which is ironic
because the closest most adults will ever come to soiling themselves
is when they attend a job interview…

This place ticks all the right wrong boxes.
Bland, soul-draining décor ✓
Air of plastic practicality ✓
Gestapo's Guide to Health and Safety ✓
Management copy of *Psychoanalysis for Dummies* ✓

I occupy the *Tough Paper-round* seat
between *Winning Smile* and *Charity Gap Year.*

First rule of Interview Club:
YOU DO NOT TALK ABOUT INTERVIEW CLUB
unless asked in the interview about Interview Club.
Second rule of Interview Club:
LEARN TO LIE.
Your eyes must show only untarnished enthusiasm.
Even the faintest flicker of weekend
will have them reaching for their trapdoor levers.

This seat was warm when I sat down.

Worry Warm or Welcome Warm?
Impossible to tell.
Probably Worry Warm.
I doubt they have staff who warm the seats.
Maybe I should mention it in the interview.

"I work well as an individual seat warmer
and as part of a team of seat warmers."

Novelty Tie's overly optimistic;
doesn't realise he's auditioning for the role of
'Disgruntled Employee No. 257'.
I tell *Charity Gap Year* that when she has a poo,
if she doesn't put the toilet seat down before she flushes,
airborne faecal matter will end up on her toothbrush.

Here comes another one;
pissed on the plonk of post interview,
positioning her face at positive angles,
but there's a *What the fuck just happened?* whisky in that walk.

Winning Smile's name is Dan.
This became apparent when someone walked past and said
"Alright Dan?"
to which he smiled and nodded.
I tell Dan that the Brown Tree Snake
is attracted to the smell of menstrual blood
and will actively seek it out.

Are there people who enjoy this?
There must be.
Maybe people who say there's no 'I' in 'Team'.
There is definitely an 'I' in 'Interrogation'.

The door to the interview room
opens in exactly the same slow motion
that loyal sidekicks use to leap in front of bullets
in Hollywood Films
and I resist the urge to shout "Nooooooooooo!!"

"David Viney."

"David Viney."

Neither a statement, nor a question.
Could it be an aptitude test?
Standard protocol seems to be to stand,
say nothing and walk solemnly into the room.
Earlier when *Wrong Shoes* replied with "Yes, that's me"
Charity Gap Year gave him the 'pity eyes'.

I stand silently,
nod solemnly
and walk towards *Yvonne with the wonky name badge on,*
convinced that she knows I ate a worm when I was two.

As I pass *Novelty Tie,*
I tell him that 15% of the air in busy Tube Stations
is human skin.

The Daily Thunk

12 MAR 2021

Poetry Gang At Large

By PAPA RATSY

Police yesterday warned the public to be vigilant, as they stepped up their hunt for the notorious Poetry Gang. Detective Inspector Keats of the Serious Rhymes Squad advised caution: "We ask that the public remain calm and do not approach this group, as they will not hesitate to use words of 3, sometimes even 4 syllables." The gang have links to prosetitution and illegal trafficking of Affable Northern Accents to unscrupulous advertising companies.

83

Facebook.
Facefeed.
Feed your face.
Book of faces.
Faces for ages.
The age of faces.
The age of familiar strangers' faces.
Hivemind.
Skivemind.
Nevermind bedtime.

Today 83% of my Facebook friends
are *Winning at Life*.
5% would 'Like' Hitler
if he posted a video of a cat playing a piano.
The rest are either on a diet that consists solely of photogenic food
or trying to steal my identity.

Just ask.
You can have it.

Facebook.
Facestalk.
You like their face, so you 'Like' their Page.
You like their face, so you 'Like' their Page.
But 'Like' a picture them from 2008?
You just graduated to Stalker mate.
Live hive.
Archive.
Give yourself a high-five.

Tomorrow I will describe tonight's poorly attended gig as follows:
The atmosphere was ubercharged.
The crowd of maybe 500, 600 people
didn't just hang on my every word,
they clung on for dear life
to the cliff edge of my brilliance.

One woman wept uncontrollably with joy.
#Humbled

Twitter this.
Twitter that.
Craft some words you lazy…
Twitter in ancient Egyptian text translates as
Gobshite.

Facebook,
face it –
at least 83% of what's said is bullshit.
At least 83% of what's *fed* is bullshit.
I mean, 83% of this *poem* is bullshit.
The rest of my life is just cats or food
or cats eating food;
I'm a raving nonsense case
since the Devil sent a Friend Request
then hacked my *actual* face!
And since you ask, it's 83 –
the percentage of time I spend stirring shit
in other people's feeds.
And if all this sounds familiar,
like you've heard all this before,
that's 'cause Facebook's been an echo chamber
since 2004,
where we like to hear opposing views
but we like our own views more.

Facebook.
Fakebook.
Fake views.
Fake news.
If it's in a meme then it must be true:
Jeremy Corbyn's beard
is a direct descendent
of Mongolian mass murderer
Genghis Khan.

Facebook,
face facts –
the future is sending a robot back
to assassinate Zuckerberg. As we speak,
it's walking with purpose down Zuckerberg's street.
It's knocking on Zuckerberg's plush front door.
Zuckerberg answers, he's pushed to the floor.
The hand in the jacket, the withdrawn gun;
Zuckerberg still doesn't know what he's done.
The laser-sight's red dot on Zuckerberg's head;
the cold lifeless eyes as the robot says…

"This is for banning cat videos in 2029."

Boom!

My English Teacher Mrs Davidson loved my writing, but thought I was a disruptive, disrespectful idiot.

She was right about the idiocy (I did a mean impression of an idiot back in the day). But I was more of a daft idiot than a disrespectful one. More deflecting than purposefully disruptive.

I spent a fair bit of Year 9 English lessons in her storage cupboard as punishment for my naïve comedic impulses. Not sure she'd get away with that these days, but I wasn't complaining. It was reasonably spacious and quiet, and ironically I took more interest in writing in that store room than I ever did in class.

Midway through each lesson, my good mate Stephen, would find an excuse to visit the storage cupboard and we would sniff poppers until our heads throbbed with the deep booming bass of boyhood stupidity. One time I left the lesson with a flashburn on my right nostril; an actual schoolboy error that saw me ridiculed mercilessly for weeks.

Truth be told I like a bit of isolation, so the punishment didn't really fit the crime. But overhearing the lack of surprise in a conversation between Ste and another of my mates in that class on my first day of incarceration remains a firm favourite of my school memories…

"Where's Dave."

"He's in the cupboard."

"Oh."

I Wanna Be Your Stuntman

I wanna to be your stuntman.

As dawn peeps over the curtains,
laughing maniacally into our mole-eyed,
boxset bingeing faces,
I wanna forward roll out of bed,
sprint across the landing
and throw myself down the stairs,
before smothering the post like a hand grenade.
Then (after a moment of medical self-assessment),
I wanna tear open the envelope marked URGENT
and joyfully proclaim…

"It's OK.
It's just a Final Warning!"

I wanna be your stuntman.

When you're sneaking into work late,
worry tugging at your features
like an anxious child on a coat sleeve.
An unidentified skiving object
on your boss's rebellion radar…
I wanna smash through your office foyer window,
engulfed in flames;
a human illumination;
a dazzling distraction,
as you slip by unnoticed
in the powder-dust smog
of several fire-extinguishers
to start your workday
30 minutes *before* you arrive.

I wanna be your stuntman.

When the Sunday supermarket hordes
pay no mind to your drum-solo hangover,
I wanna co-opt the security guard,
throw the first air-punch
and invoke the spirit of a Hollywood Western,
as a blurred, tangle of sham-angry customers
play-fight by the self-service tils –
fake sugar-glass condiment bottles
smashing over heads,
kicks that don't connect,
fists that don't land –
assaulting only the cool conditioned air around them,
while across the store
you hazily contemplate comfort food
in the comfort of your own aisle.

I wanna be your stuntman.

When the cinematic storm
mumbles its advance apology
and the washing line weather report
is thunderpants and isobras…
when your Saturday night garms are in harm's way,
I wanna leap from a first floor window
onto a pile of conveniently placed cardboard boxes,
catch an angry, baffled cat
thrown by an overzealous stunt co-ordinator
and deflect an in-flight phoney fence panel,
before plucking those clothes to safety
like they were toddlers
in the path of a runaway bin lorry.

I wanna be your stuntman.

I want that falling ten stories minimum love;
that real hurricane, not a wind-tunnel love;
that fighting on top of express trains love;
that cling to a wing of a jet plane love;
that flipping a car doing 80 love;
that jump from explosion to safety love;
that swim through a flooded compartment love;
that gunned down by Hollywood hardmen love.
And when I'm past all that perilous things type love,
it can still be a take out the bins type love.
But for now

I wanna be your stuntman.

Stretford is, I suppose, my 'home town'.

It's picture-postcard. If the picture is a drunk fighting a pigeon and the postcard's got a corner missing where it's been used for roach. It's the kind of place the Council take the glass out of bus-stops, just to cut out the middle man.

Stretford's always refused to be gentrified. But Stretford is a neighbour to areas that have tried gentrification, with varying levels of success...

Chorlton: where it's no longer enough to be 100% organic human organism – you have to be at least 70% kale. You may think they're turning their noses up at you... they're not, they're sniffing for kale. I actually applaud their efforts at European-esque outdoor spaces. But some of the bars in Chorlton are so close to busy roads that when you order shots from the outside seating area, they bring you a tray of asthma inhalers. Two-for-one cocktails? "I'll have a Sex On The Beach and Carbon Monoxide Poisoning On Patio Furniture please."

Urmston: where you can now get glassed by sixteen different types of craft ale. Burnt out Ocado van... e-bike in a tree... a memorial bench with a plaque that reads *In Memory of Gaz, who tried to explain Facial Toner to his mates down the pub*. The warning signs are there though – they have a cheese shop. Their market is now 'Artisan'. The beer glasses are looking more and more like vases.

Sale: the Wild West of gentrification... big bales of kale blowing down the high street, sustainably sourced saloon doors creaking in the breeze, unkempt beards as far as the eye can see, a posse of scalpers cutting top-knots off unsuspecting hipsters. Sale has all the ingredients for gentrification – good looking pubs by a canal, its own arts centre, good amenities and restaurants... but Sale has a not-so-secret weapon up its sleeve in the fight against gentrification – the lairy drinker. The kind that smokes Benson & Hedges ironically because Bensons is a bed shop, but Hedge is where they'll end up spending the night. The boozy advances of Bingo Brian, a hit with the ladies at the local Mecca – lock up your dotters.

But Stretford, so far, has resisted gentrification...

All the Same to Stretford

You can tear down its historic Hall
which we commandeered to drink and smoke.
You can overdub its subway walls
with High School murals and Old School quotes.
You can tell it the Arndale's now a Mall,
where Metrosexuals mingle with 'blokes'.

It's all the same to Stretford.

You can give it a tram for its old train tracks.
You can talk of its future, but not of its past.
You can make apartments out of its flats.

It's all the same to Stretford.

You can call its outskirts Chorlton Border,
where the outside tables / outside chairs
give the bars a feel of Farcelona
as you drink in heavy traffic air.
You can tell it that it's out of order
for its general lack of social care;
that it's part school bully, part stoned loner,
partly urban park warfare.

Yeah, it's all the same to Stretford.

You can talk of its regeneration,
like some sad dishevelled Doctor Who.
But even Daleks risk extermination
on the Number 22*

You can speak of ten-year murder rates
and point out it's had two,
but while it's got a touch of drive-by,
it's still more of a drive-through.

You can pimp its park with a posh café.
You can pay a Fat Cat for a Skinny Latte.
But you can't contain your horror, as little Oliver plays
with that kick-off kid who's going through a *difficult stage*.

But hey, it's all the same to Stretford.

You can renovate a council house
and buy a Four-by-Four.
You can have organic vegetables
delivered to your door.
You can choose a quiet cul-de-sac,
but you'll still hear the roar
of some battered Nissan Micra
with a fucking sports exhaust!

That one grates a bit on Stretford.

Here Ye Apple Mac Creatives,
Dapper Gents and Bo Ho Ladies…
Homes are selling fast just lately;
In a state, but could be Stately.
Weeding out the common daily,
It's a case of when, not maybe.
Transport Links? The trains are gravy!
Catchment Area's amazing!
Move in now and have smart babies.
Up and coming…

since the eighties.

It's all the same to Stretford.

* The Stagecoach Bus Company has now changed the No. 22 to the No. 25 – but I'm not letting the facts get in the way of a perfectly good rhyme.

The revolution will not be televised

It will be on Zoom

SadOh

My friend tells me he thinks he has '**SAD D**isorder'.
I tell him that the **S.A.D.** stands for
Seasonal **A**ffective **D**isorder,
so if he has **SAD** *Disorder*
that means he has
Seasonal **A**ffective **D**isorder **D**isorder.
I tell him he probably has
Shit at **A**cronyms **D**isorder.
He tells me that doesn't even work as an acronym.
I tell him that just makes it funnier.
He tells me I might have
Sarcastic **A**rsehole **D**isorder.
I ask him if he means
Sarcastic **A**rsehole **D**isorder **D**isorder?

That was a while ago.
We don't talk much now.

I'm not punching down with that joke by the way – I have S.A.D. (no, the Seasonal one) and I live in Manchester, so if anything it's a figurative uppercut to my own pasty, melancholy mug.

Buttons

She has [insert insufficient superlative here] eyes
that can steal speech from cocksure mouthpieces
and blind off-guard, foolhardy soul searchers.
A heart in hiding.
Maybe when the bruising goes down.
Approaches trust like a firework.
Knows that if it explodes only she will feel it.
Knows because it has.
Frisks compliments for concealed weapons,
and her walls…
Her walls are reinforced
with solid resolve,
topped with shards
of bro ken promises.

He trips over the darkness of darker days.
Overshares, unaware that he's purging.
Remembers just a moment too late
that not all childhoods were made this way,
but refuses not to cherish the blisters:
pantomimes his past,
acts like audience –
ridicules his villains.

She patents infectious angle-finding;
knows the shape of hustle.
Splashes through conversations like puddles.
Laughs with no pretext, subtext or contest.
Tries to face-pull beauty away, but fails
beautifully.

He is an open book
in a locked box.
Hug-pushes affection to a safe distance.
Feels unbalanced, fogged-up –
waits for her to scrawl her name in his condensation.

They love in radar blips;
near misses on the grid.
Laugh in parallel.
Settle into the thought of each other
like freshly washed sheets.
Peripherally aware that if they ever aligned
their shared memories would over time
become soft focus,
accompanied by a button-pushing power ballad
that neither would own up to.

Face Value (Part 1)

Let's dispense with the pleasantries shall we.
Let's not fuck around –
this Britain is the face of Two Thousand and Now.
It has no time to be nice.
Your small-talk isn't small enough.
This poem is on a clock,
attached to a bomb,
shaped like a watch.

What it's trying to tell you
is that it doesn't have time to explain
what it's trying to tell you.

This poem has a keen ear;
hears the penny drop;
knows the instant gratification is in danger of lingering –
it's starting to stink the place up.
You can't react fast enough to be relevant.
The E.U. elephant in the room,
with wolves at the door.
The Payday-Pauper, status-infatuated.
This Britain is overwhelmed and oversaturated –
housebound, plugged in,
boxing the shadow of the Britain it could have been
and if you even think…

about pausing…

this Britain will be on you in a newsflash
to remind you that the Earth is still spinning
at 460 metres per second.
We're all dying at 3600 seconds per hour.

Nuclear grade sadness and frustration
threatens to destroy the planet at any moment,
but the word on the street is
do more
sleep less
drink more coffee
– exhaustion is the fast-track to success.
Have your breakdown in your own time though,
so there's no Domino Effect.
All that we expect from you
is nothing less than perfect.

Oh, and… no pressure.

This Britain is the face of Two Thousand and Now
and thanks to advances in data analysis
it has the measure of you.
It has already buttered you up
and cut you into convenient bite-sized chunks.
It has categorised you, satirised you
and patronised you.
It knows your *kind*.
It's had dealings with your demographic.
It keeps you on a memory card,
inside a box,
inside a safe,
inside a vault,
inside an impregnable fortress,
because as much as it wants to sound like you,
your existence makes it ill
and it prays you never breed.

This Britain can't get worked up about impoverished families.
But is absolutely incensed by slow broadband speed.

Juggling its ethics with two balls
and a juggernaut –
this Britain is brought to you by Beauty Incorporated:
the manufacture of imperfection to generate wealth;
a surgical incision to our collective mental health;
the expressionless face;
the immovable brow;
this Britain is the face of Two Thousand and Now.

It knows the revolution's coming.
But it's fucked if it knows how

because it's a keyboard warrior, brat-pack blogger,
Twitterati, late to the party revolutionary.
It solves nothing.
But it does it across multiple media platforms
to an audience of equally enraged inactivists.

This Britain is the clenched fist of Resistance,
inside the pocket of a jacket,
hand-stitched for a pittance
to maximise profit.

This Britain is not equipped with the empathy you ask of it.
This Britain wants to know 'What's in it for me?'
This Britain carries the guns for an elitist killing spree.
This Britain expects that it will all just get better somehow.

This Britain is the face of Two Thousand and Now.

Face Value (Part 2): This Time It's Personal

Let's dispense with the formalities shall we.
Let's all gather round –
This Britain is the face of Two Thousand and Now.
It makes the time to be nice.
Your small-talk is a pathway to large scale social change.
This Britain is on the streets,
attached to compassion,
shaped like signatures in concrete.

What it's trying to tell you
*is that people are **dying** for you to hear*
what it's trying to tell you.

This Britain has a keen ear;
hears the voiceless drop
into the grinding gears of economy and progress;
a machine that never stops.
It can't compact fast enough – they're irrelevant;
the see-through elephant in the room,
with wolves at the door.
The Payday-Pauper. Status is fabricated.
This Britain is overwhelmingly over hatred.
Housebound, plugged in,
boxing the shadow of the cabinet that boxed it in.
And if you even think…

about pausing…

this Britain will be on you with Hobnobs
to remind you that the Earth is still spinning thanks to gravity.
It is not a 460 metres per second hamster wheel.

We may be dying at 3600 seconds per hour,
but we are living at 84,600 seconds per day
and though nuclear grade sadness and frustration
threaten to destroy the planet at any moment,
the despair in our hearts can be diffused,
so
do more good
sleep less restless
share more coffee
– community is the fast track to success.
Have your breakdown in a supermarket though,
fuck the Domino Effect!
All that we expect from you
is to be perfectly imperfect.

And genuinely… no pressure.

This Britain is the face of Two Thousand and Now
and thanks to advances in data analysis
it has the measure of them.
It has already laid scent to their deceit
and let loose a bloodhound that never needs sleep.
It has tracked them, hacked them
and counter-attacked them.
It knows their *kind*.
It's had dealings with their demographic.
It sees them in dark corners of contempt,
inside a scam,
inside a travesty,
inside a paid for peerage,
inside a fortress of status,
because as much as they want to sound like truth,
they exist only to get their fill
and they pray to gods of greed.

This Britain is incensed that impoverished families
are talked about less than broadband speed.

Juggling its self-worth with two balls
and a juggernaut –
this Britain is brought to you by Beauty Recalibrated:
breaking down stigma around mental health.
A helping hand for all, no matter what hand they were dealt;
the welcoming face;
next up / next gen;
this Britain will be better in Two Thousand and Then.

It knows the revolution's coming
and that *it* decides when

because it's a people worrier, back-pack slogger,
Twitter-fuckin' arsey, let's have a party revolutionary.
It involves EVERYONE
and it does it across multiple media platforms
to an audience of equally engaged collectivists.

This Britain is the clenched fist of Resistance,
extended to the heavens, rejecting their pittance
and their elitist Armageddon.

This Britain is fully equipped with empathy – 24/7.
This Britain wants to know 'How can I help?'
This Britain's of a mind to redistribute the wealth.
This Britain bends the knee, but will not bow.

This Britain is the face of Two Thousand and Now.

Mum used to iron crazy creases
into my clothes.
Aeroplane sleeves. Heptagon jeans.

Looking back on it now, I think
she was telling me it was time
to do my own ironing.
She'd say I looked a million dollars.

But we both knew I looked a pound...
50 Pence per leg.

Then …

There's a wet winter's day in my veins
and then
life is seeming completely in vain
and then
I'm hiring a soul that can cope
and then
I'm dreading the hymns about hope
and then
the wait wears you down over weeks
and then
the funeral's a fucking relief
and then
my chest forgets that it should breathe
and then
the trees bow their branches in grief
and then
the clouds have a right good old weep
and then
time as a concept just stops
and then
a relative looks at their watch
and then
it's hands clasped and eyes on the floor
and then
it's done and all eyes on the door
and then
it's just me who feels the ground shake
and then
the walls crumbling, falling away
and then
cracks in the dam of my mind
and then

I'm flooded with you in your prime
and then
bodies with warm blood embrace
and then
no one has a face that's your face
and then
Love's spell defaults to a curse
and then
my heart leaves in that empty hearse
and then
the wake is a truth told in eyes
and then
the stories told border on lies
and then
alcohol feeds me my lines
and then
Grief rings the bell and calls time
and then
the last of the well-wishers leaves
and then
the only one wishing is me
and then…

That'll Learn 'em

Lost for Words

A univocalism using only one vowel throughout – 'o'.

Pods sown.
From pod root grows.
From root wood forms.
From wood book born.
Book holds words…
Strong words…
Strong words blossom to form strong story.
Book holds strong story.
Plot not lost.
Strong story told to world, only…
Woods lost to words.
Woods don't root for books.
Woods, monsoon moody – roots torn, storm off.
Vow to knock off work pronto –
Down tools…

Job's off.

Woods cool down.
Frown shook off
Woods form shop:
Shopfront – Bold Font:
Booksnotfromwood.com
Boom!
Lots of loot.
Good old woods
know now not to worry.
Strong words blossom to form strong story.
Booksnotfromwood shoots to glory – tons sold.
Strong story told to world.
Wow!
Woods lost for words.

Poem Upon Seeing an Ex in a Bar When You've Just Finished Teaching Poetry Techniques*

Rhyming:	Can't say I miss you. I wish you were near. The urge is to kick you, to kiss you – the fear
Repetition:	is that love is a cycle of repeated mistakes, that love is recycled, repeated – mistake.
Onomatopoeia:	You truth-biurt – unburden, shush-comfort with hug.
Alliteration:	You've a tale-twister's talent – turn tears into truces
Assonance:	but your wars are all fought with the thought of poor you –
Simile:	you fight like a boxer who's too fond of bruises.
Metaphor:	Your eyes are murals to a once vibrant soul,
Hyperbole:	defaced by an infinite graffiti of excuses.
Symbolism:	Now your white flags are red rags – do not approach. You haven't pulled. I'll get your coat.

* Yeah, it's niche.

What Donald Did Next

An Abecedarian poem / A-Z.

"Absolute assholes!" he screams, defeated.
Beaten by decency.
Can't think of anything more…
Disgusting!
Exit through the gift shop.
Fuck you very much.
Goes straight to bed, eyes leaking.
Has that same hot recurring dream:
Initiate nuclear holocaust.
Jam all communications.
Kill all Commies.
Look up 'Messiah' – picture of him, obviously.
Make history a thing of the past.
Nukes are GO.
Only select few soon. Must have
Putin over to bunker for tea.
Queen not so much.
Respect is a one-way street.
Shoot all dissidents.
That's the way Kimmy does it.
Ultimate power.
Very sexual.
"Wait 'til they get a load o' me!"
X-Rated, dictated – greatest world ever!
Yes, Mr President, we have achieved Ground
Zero.

My Classes Wear Invisible Glasses

For Year 5 / Year 6 pupils of Charlestown and Unity Community Primary Schools and their excellent minds.

My classes wear invisible glasses
that show empathy and culture
and community and the future
in great detail.
My classes tell me tales
of no pollution,
an end to discrimination.
My classes wear invisible glasses
that show them solutions.
You don't need glasses to see my classes'
determination.

My classes wear invisible glasses
that give them a group vision
of less division and more unity.
My classes' invisible glasses are new to me.
See my invisible glasses are old now,
they don't fold well now
and they need a good clean.
But through my classes' invisible glasses,
I can see dreams.

I can see sky-high excitement –
A galaxy of Great, filled with shining stars of Hope.
My classes' invisible glasses
are more powerful than telescopes.

My classes wear invisible glasses,
which show them kindness and caring.

My classes' invisible glasses
prevent blindness to suffering when wearing.
So don't go unspoken if your glasses are broken
and the cold light of day seems too glaring.
Because my classes wear invisible glasses
and my classes don't mind sharing.

Insert picture of glasses here. DV.

Already have. Ed.

Things that should definitely happen #2
MICK HUCKNALL SHOULD RECORD A POETRY COLLECTION AND CALL IT ...
Simile Red
52X
CD-R
700MB 80MIN

No Wonder

Aimed at the haters, not the debaters.

It's no wonder you're tired –
you've been dealing with the hoodoo, voodoo,
supposedly clued-up conspiracy theorists,
spontaneous miscellaneous mouthpieces,
tin-foil hat Kerouacs;
the ones who'd rather cuss you than have a discussion.
The ones who've managed to *solve the world*
from the comfort of their living room.
Codshit fishermen
who'll tell you that you've been reeled in
for believing in compassion –
the unfashionable, unfathomable notion of caring for strangers.

But unfortunately
you've always wondered what makes a sociopath tick,
so you ask them how they reach their conclusions.
Where they fish for answers.
Where they cast their nets.

And they say,
"The internet."

You say, "The internet?
Invented by humans and therefore entirely corruptible.
That internet?"

And without a hint of irony they say,
"Yeah."

It's as unwise to fact-check conspiracy theories on the internet
as it is to ask a conspiracy theorist for directions –

"Excuse me mate, could you tell me how to get to Jackson Street…?"
"Do your own research!"

If you're a fan of the online exposé that can't reveal its source
then you've run into more fake webs than Harrison Ford.
You've seen more shite than an out of favour sewage worker.

No one's saying approach life blindly.
But some guiding lights are provided by snipers.
Some light-bulb moments attract killer moths.

I agree, the bigger picture *is* photoshopped;
the portrait of a civilised society does not reflect the people.
The smiles are added in after
and the souls are airbrushed to hide the evil.

But the discovery of a worldwide conspiracy
played out in memes and petty insults on social media…

You don't think that's a little bit too convenient?

And now browsing the internet is like bobbing for apples
in a deep fat fryer.

Remember when we had time?
Remember when we used it for mindless fun
that was still more worthwhile
than this endless, soulless mojo-sapping diatribe.
And yeah, we nearly died.
But we did it with smiles on our faces,
in union, with conviction
and watched our beautifully flawed humanity
step off a cliff and spread its wings.

But that was before you called me a prick on social media.

So now I'm sat here seething
in the lonely glow of my hypnotic phone screen
and it's no wonder I'm tired –

following the complex plot of what's what.
Am I really conversing with the BOTS of the Have-a-lots?
Are there really automated programmes
posting comments on social media?

Back in the day,
talk of Skynet and Terminators seemed outrageous.
But now it's hard to tell if Karen's a human
or a robot racist.

And don't worry if the landscape of society is unrecognisable
and daily atrocities fail to raise an eyebrow,
because eyebrow raising is on its way out…

Not long now before we're Botox'd at Birth, surely…
Not long now before we're spared the sight
of those hideous teenage wrinklies…
Not long now before we replace facial expressions with emoji masks
of varying quality, depending on our financial clout…

"I'm absolutely gutted,"
says the girl with Blu Tack eyes and downturned marker pen mouth,
and it's no wonder she's tired…

…by the search for emotionally intelligent humans.
Not mercenaries dressed as civilians.
Marjorie's a sweetheart at work,
but of an evening, she's a menace to sobriety –
can type 65 words per minute
all of the xenophobic variety.

And it's no wonder Marjorie's tired…
What with the hardening of her veins and the hardening of her heart
and all the things the papers tell her she should be angry about.
But she can't do as the subtle heckler does –
be a more refined hater,
build a Trojan Horse from rose-tinted spectacles,
fill it with the weaponised headlines of mainstream newspapers
and leave it to be taken in
by the confounded townspeople of *I'mnotracistbut,*
a snide British town
twinned with the bigoted Russian Mining village of *Korsh Yurnot.*
And it's no wonder they're all tired,
because I wrote them that way
and because all roads lead to road.
In a matrix of corrupt equations
the value of life has never changed,
it's always been worth less than money.
But now we've reduced scientific endeavour
to any online loon in an on-loan lab coat…
Science fact or science fiction?
says social media with its PHD in Pish.
We've reduced history to a constant stream
of inaccurate 'facts' and misquote memes…

In the words of the late, great Martin Luther King:
Mankind – what a bunch of dicks!

PANTOMIND
Where's the generation picking up the pieces?
They're behind you!

Partly Political Broadcast

Warning!
This is a Partly Political Broadcast.
Due to increasing division in communities
over Brexit, which political party you support,
masks, no masks, pandemic, plandemic,
and whether cruel is the new rock n' roll,
it is now entirely plausible to HATE YOUR FRIENDS.

Yes, you will hate your friends.
But you will not *act* like you hate your friends,
because they are your friends
and you've known them for 'like, forever'.
And you love them, but you…
Well, you don't actually *hate* them –
it's just that sometimes when they talk,
you find yourself retching at the putrid stench
of the bile that flows like toxic waste
from the distended rectum where their face used to be.
BUT you remember when they had a face
and that you liked that face,
and that good things came out of that face.

And you know, maybe there's some form of exorcism
for people who've lost all their empathy –
like tying them to a bed
and reading them the Metro's Newspaper's *Good Deed Feed…*
Warning!
Their head will spin like an eight-year-old in a revolving door.
Their projectile vomit will cover the ceiling and the walls.
But on the plus side,
their soul will be purged of the evil within.

Or maybe you're the one tied *to* the bed,
fingers loosening the knots at your wrists.
Tuning out your soft-arse mate, 'cause ignorance is bliss.
Enjoying the thought of overpowering
that Lefty liberal streak of piss...
Warning!
Do not force them to listen
to your reworked right-wing Christmas hits
like 'I'm Dreaming of an Exclusively White Christmas',
'Left Nuts Roasting on an Open Fire'
or 'Snowflakes Falling on a Cold Hard Boot'.

These examples are purposefully extreme.
But our division is the fetish
in every capitalist's wet dream.

Congratulations!
You are now BFF's –
Best Friends Fornever.

Social gatherings will be a minefield of trigger-words
and conversational click-bait.
Build a diplomacy moat in your mind
between yourself and the friend that you love / hate the most.
Fill it with reminders of when you actually liked each other:
images of shared idols, music that united you,
drugs that wore you like demented sock puppets.
Warning!
Do NOT remove the drugs from the diplomacy moat.
Warning!
Put the drugs BACK in the moat.
Warning!
Do NOT take the drugs FROM the moat
WITH the friends that you love / hate.

Warning!
Do NOT 'forward slash' anyone.

You are now the best of Frienemies.
Conversations between you will be more awkward
than a church group meeting in the basement of a swingers' club.

Listening to a Frienemy's views on immigration
will be like a duel with water-pistols, filled with warm piss –
no one will die.
But you will never be able to untaste that one drop
that rolled down your cheek and into the corner of your mouth.

Drinks with a Frienemy should be approached with caution;
Remember, there's a reason they drink water and not Tequila
at United Nations meetings.

Never ever play Monopoly with a Frienemy.

The *Looney Left* (represented by *Wheelbarrow, Thimble, Boot*)
will purchase hotels
and turn them into hippy communes,
squandering their cash on namby-pamby, arty-farty
social change initiatives
like affordable housing
and youth engagement!
All their Chance Cards *will be* JAIL –
for pointless causes like protesting for a stranger's human rights,
or blockading a Fracking Site on Old Kent Road.

The *Rabid Right* (represented by *Battleship, Racing Car, Top Hat*)
will confiscate all the Community Chest Cards;
there is only one valid community
and that is *their* non-communal community.

And Chance Cards – they're for losers,
because winners make their own luck.
Remember that what you own defines you.
Warning!
If you were childhood friends, go directly home.
Do not pass 'GO Fuck Yourself'.
Do not collect 200 potential counter-arguments
to change their mind.
Any player who is financially bankrupt, loses.
Any player who is emotionally bankrupt, loses.
The Bank *never* loses.

Warning…

The *Filthy Rich* will never be filthy or rich enough.

Blood

Mum,
today I build a podium
from all the doors that you tore through with sarcasm
when circumstance slammed them in your face.
From the shelves stacked with sacrifices
that you stored in the basement of yourself
and the financial planks you walked
with loan sharks circling below.

The nails will be forged from the melted-down cannon ball odds
that you restacked to shout over their walls.

The banner, hand-stitched from the bedlinen roofs
of the couch cushion forts that you project managed,
will display one word in Building Block Font:

UNFLINCHING

and below it, a trestle table
crafted from the park benches
that we sat on to ponder the world together
will strain under the weight of all the trophies
I should have given you.
They will be BIG – to incorporate the inscriptions:

Best Mum at sneaking into school at 8am
when I forget my homework
so we can do it together over breakfast

Best mum at getting me off the bus
and seeing me across the road

while standing in front of the bus
so that the driver has to wait
and you don't lose your job for being late

Best mum at having the last word –
5 times champion at drawing gasps from well-to-do mums

Best mum at wrapping my school books in woodchip wallpaper
so they will survive in times of nuclear holocaust

Best mum at turning a 5 foot 3 height disadvantage
into a 9 foot 9 dressing down

Best Lioness in the Pride

Best Pride by a good mum's mile
which is 2,456 miles long

Best when tested

Best at being unimpressed by aggressive

A backlash of balloons will be released
into an ill-prepared pacifist's sky –
each carrying a letter that you penned
with hand-written righteousness and boiled-blood ink
for anyone and everyone who needed your help,
returning final demands with demands of your own.
To this day,
councilmen still back into corners, clutching letter-openers
at the mere mention of your name.

Of course, I have booked a stand-in stunt-double
to spare you from the fuss that you cannot
and will not tolerate.

She will wear an applause-proof vest,
a wig of your choosing
and a wry smile to complete the illusion.
It will be the biggest party we've never attended…

sat in your flat,
restacking the odds,
pondering the world together.

* * *

Dad,
Today I build a time-machine
from the scattered fragments of landmines
that you laid in your own path.
From the medals of dishonour I pinned upon you
before we diffused each other's rage
and the gold stars you earned thereafter.
From the enigma we decoded
and the allied code we co-created.

Today I salvage parts from your archives
 – early '70s –
when watches stopped ticking and started humming
when their inner balance wheels
made way for batteries and crystals –
you harboured a heart with slipping gears,
a coiled spring where your stomach should have been
and cogs that if wound into action
would set off a series of death-defying traps,
poison-tipped spear pits and giant boulders –
as would later be witnessed by Indiana Jones in '81.
You must have had a really bad day that day.

The Quantum Core will be cobbled together
from the cars you showed up in when I was a kid –
who says a time-machine can't be part Nissan Bluebird?
It will be powered by the infamous frenetic energy of your fists;
the fairground boxer, the boxed-in scrapper.
The fearless defender.
The dadyoudon'tmesswith.
But also the capacity of your kindness,
the unstoppable momentum of your problem solving
and whatever it is they call that spark behind the eyes.

Our time-jump will not be instantaneous though –
I will programme a 20-minute delay
to honour your ETA for every emergency,
no matter the distance.
'The Twenty Minute Man' –
saviour of sons with no sense.
The first stop will be my 9th birthday,
a card from me to me, unsigned,
three words:

Give it time xx

* * *

Brother,
Today I build a toll bridge
from the remains of all the bridges that came before it.
From the incendiary surroundings of our sibling rivalry.
Somewhere, masked by the clamour of falling masonry
there is a sonic signature;
two boys in matching pyjamas…
Sofa Island. Shark infested carpet.
Me – the water-winged lifeguard, out of his depth.

You – unaware the tide is rising.
We of Television Eyes and weightless of world,
as concrete and steel rain down around us.

I collect scraps;
plunder junkyards of non-starters and write-offs,
wade through crushed peace pipes and broken olive branches,
examine corroded memories for traces of *once*.

Today I struggle for materials.

Today I struggle for words.

Today I am the wrong man for this job.

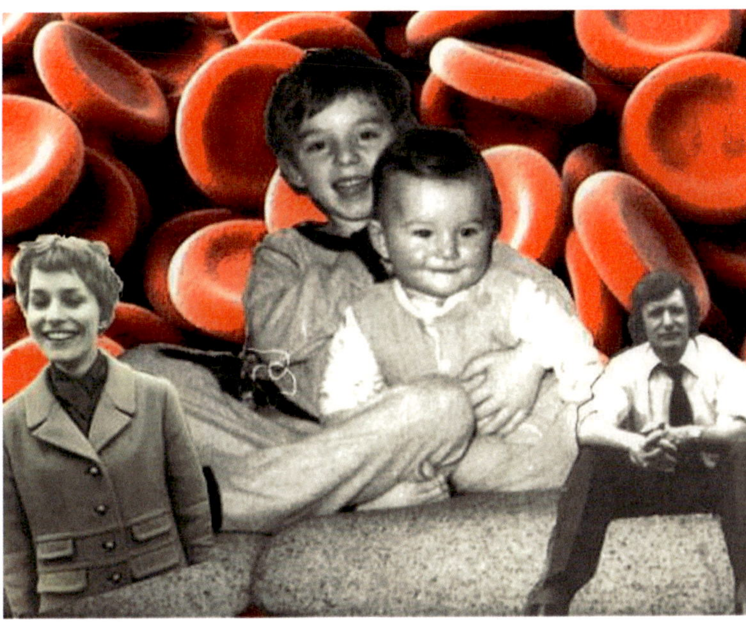

Heavyweight Champion of the World

When I woke up this morning
my nose didn't fit.
My body-shape was diabolical,
so I rearranged it.
My skin tone was incompatible
with this day and age;
you must exude sunshine,
not a rainy shade of grey.
I settled on transparency.
I wish I hadn't done it,
for there I saw my heavy heart
with the weight of the world upon it.

Practising poems
on cats ...

The Walk of ~~Shame~~ Acclaim

Today – heads heavy as aeroplanes.
Today – belly a carousel of foreign items.
Today – Home / Bed / Sanctuary…
DELAYED / DELAYED / DELAYED
Today we touch down like The Beatles.
Today the walk of shame is repackaged,
relabelled, rereleased to critical acclaim.

Today our hangover tells us it is bigger than God.

And we believe.

Today our arrival sees the crowd swell.
Reporters, desperate for a glimpse of regret,
fantasise our engine failure.
Fans silently mime their screams of adulation.
A sponsorship deal with Aspirin
is a mere formality.

We are finally, unreservedly adored.

It is the least we deserve.

Yesterday – the momentum of crash-test bodies
and crumpled frames.
Yesterday – whiplash interactions and
unpredictable impacts.
Yesterday we crashed, we burned,
we sculpted ourselves from ash.
Yesterday – all my troubles seemed…

DELAYED.

Marry Me

Marry me in a sci-fi church,
if you're sure the vicar will materialise.
And if I fall in with the wrong crowd,
marry me in the company of cast iron alibis.

Marry me in a Las Vegas chapel,
with star-spangled inflatable pews.
Chinese Elvis can perform the ceremony
to the rhythm of 'Blue Suede Shoes'.

Propose to me, exposed to me.
Get a heavy fine imposed for me.

Marry me on the handlebars
of a rustic Raleigh Chopper,
on a bruised and battered skateboard
or a faded space-hopper.

Propose to me, foreclose for me.
Have an ex-lover's lair bulldozed for me.

Marry me in fancy tags.
We'll sell it to the glossy mags.
Your mum caught out with crafty fag.
The hard up hats and fake handbags.
The best forgotten Best Man gags.
The Hens all eyeing up the Stags.
The Stags all breaking out their brags.
We'll tell our story – all we've blagged.
We're rags to riches…

riches to rags.

Marry me in a haunted house.
Well, we know you love your spirits.
And if my soul sells to the highest bidder,
ghost me and marry my harshest of critics.

Marry me in the murderous glare
of your soon-to-be-a-convict dad.
On reflection I wouldn't have told him
that you're an unbelievable shag.

Propose to me, dispose of me.
Recycle – make the most of me.

Marry me Saturday, 2am
on the lairy top deck of the 86.
We'll stumble haphazardly down the aisle,
as confetti is switched for chicken shop chips.

Propose to me, compose for me.
Send a letter through to the post to me.

Your dad says it's the thought that counts.
Says you can't buy happy marriages.
Says he knows a guy who does half-dead horse-drawn
rust-encrusted carriages.
Says he feeds the horses Pick 'n' Mix
at 24-hour garages.

So let's celebrate.

Let's celebrate the kind of love
that makes the birds sing
and the sun come out.
The kind of love that makes people cringe
and be a little sick in their mouth.

Because fuck it if they're sour-faced
and fuck their ruined appetite
and fuck it if we have pet names,
my Little Fluffy Parasite.
Fuck their smug percentages
and fuck their bleak statistics
and fuck their tainted hearts,
when they say we're not realistic.
And fuck it if it falls apart.

Divorce me, with one promise…

It's pretty expensive this marriage lark.
Marry me again in a Registrar's Office.

Bon Jovial

ARCHERY CLUB
Shot through the heart and you're to blame.
Darling, you give archery centres a bad name.

HAPPY 18th BIRTHDAY OLIVER
HAPPY 30th SEBASTIAN
Things that should definitely happen #3
PUTTING FAKE BIRTHDAY MESSAGES ON TRAFFIC ROUNDABOUTS IN AFFLUENT AREAS

They spend their days
lurking in the shadows –
rapid aperture eyes.
Shutter speed blink
captures the moment
you definitely don't want developed
into an open-mic reveal.

Big Scooper.
Short-hand Shakespeare.
Nuclear notepad.

Subdued by the glare of their imagination,
you agree to an exclusive.

The headline reads

This One's Called My Ex Likes Coldplay

Asking me to say
things in a
straightforward
way

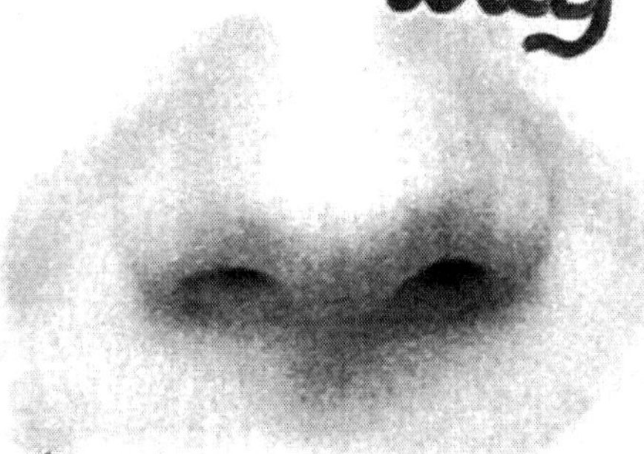

gets up my
nasal
apparatus

Todaydreamer

Tomorrow's To-do List:

- Command your thoughts;
  relax to the drastic.
  Use a sanity you made earlier
  with sticky-back plastic.

- Buy competitively-priced novelty goods;
  bin the boring and the plain.

  See the world
  through rose-tinted cellophane.

- Be a used-hope salesman
  selling second-hand desires.
  Booby-trap all conversations…
  wait for the crossed wires.

- Duck, dive and hustle
  through tricky situations.
  Scoop yourself a Pick 'n' Mix
  of life's sweetest persuasions.

- Work for stress, low pay and a Molotov Migraine.
  (Still be standing room only on the 07:18 Gravy Train).

- Be food for thought,
  eat humble pie,
  be a couch potato,
  be the apple of your eye.
  Be crackers.

  Dry.

- Make Hopscotch compulsory
  for overbearing dads.
  Prove him wrong and punch your way
  out of that paper bag.

- Seek out spoilers on your future.
  Get the drop on Fate's intentions.
  Mystic Margaret sees it all
  and needs a new extension.

- Make todaydreams your reality.
  Give the nightmares the heave-ho.
  There won't always be a crock of shit
  at the end of every rainbow.

Today's To-do List:

- See tomorrow.

The final poem in this collection, 'Our City', was written in two parts.

I originally set about writing a poem about my home city that wasn't re-treading the same Manchester themes covered so well by other Mancunian poets like Marvin Cheeseman, Mike Garry or Tony Walsh among others, so I tried to capture the spirit of the place and the people in a way that I'd experienced it personally.

Then the Arena bombing happened and like most Mancunians I didn't have the words. I was resigned to leaving the poem half finished, until I could think clearly – and even then I thought it might not happen. It was only after I'd watched the One Love Manchester concert on TV that I knew I had to finish it. The image of those kids rejecting hate and symbolising hope is one that has stayed with me. It took a while after, and there's always a worry that you won't represent in the right way. But the response has been really positive.

I've since collaborated with the excellent band Narcissus to put the poem to music, which is on the charity album from Mancmade, *Acts of Hope* (highly recommend purchasing a copy via 42's Records) – a lot of the tracks were put together specifically for the record and all funds go to the charity. There are tracks by Peter Hook and Johnny Marr on there amongst others.

There are a couple of versions of this poem knocking about due to collaborations and edits, but this is the version you're getting ☺ – it's shamelessly sentimental, as all love poems should be.

Our City

In our city
you can see *sound.*

Our city's never had a Tube,
but always had an underground.

Our city's a Masterclass of past masters,
unsurpassed in the art of
Choons
(spelt with an imperative CH).

Our city's always led the way,
so technically we're never late.

Our city can be outshone,
but never outdone.

Our city's billed as Number 2,
but knows it's Number 1.

When visiting be sure to pack correctly for your stay –
our city has been known to have
four seasons in one day.

You see, our city likes a raincloud,
but our city isn't bleak.
It's been said that all our city's missing
is a beach.

In our city
there's a Preacher Man in every Indie Club.
His emblem is a Bee and his true calling is a buzz.

He says that "Heaven's a loop of the 1989 Summer of Love."
He'll tell you tales of angels wearing baggy jeans and happy hoods.
But Manchester knows angels wear nurse uniforms and scrubs.

Because our city speaks in actions.
Our city rallies round;
50,000 danced defiant in our city's cricket ground.
And who didn't shed a tear (or ten)
as the cameras scanned the crowd
and then the faces of those kids in rapture;
signs held high proclaiming LOVE,
not hate, not anger.
Their choked-back tears and hopeful laughter;
Grande's grand and heartfelt gesture...
it felt like it did lasting good.

50,000 beaming faces.
Beamed to over *100 million* places.

A message that will long resound
on giant screens, in fearless sound;
the Mancs have put a marker down –

you won't divide and conquer us.
We're not that kind of town.

It's simple:
our city does do *Bez Dancing, Talking to Strangers,*
The Art of Sarcasm and *Pioneers*.
Our city doesn't do *taking itself too seriously, Vitamin D,*
hatred, division or *fear*.

As Anthony H. Wilson said when asked about his peers:
"This is Manchester. We do things differently here."

BONUS FEATURES

DEAD ALERT
BY
DAVID VINEY

A 3-minute play written for Rapid Reel in response to Boris Johnson's 'Stay Alert' press conference.

During lockdown Rapid Reel tasked writers to respond to a news story within 24 hours, then sourced an actor to bring the script to life.

Starring Jack Gogarty

Released 11th May 2020

youtu.be/22I-TUBPg2Y

SCENE: INT. JIMMY'S KITCHEN.

LIGHTS UP

WE ARE LOOKING INTO A KITCHEN VIA WEBCAM ON JIMMY'S LAPTOP WHICH IS ON THE KITCHEN COUNTER.

JIMMY COMES INTO SHOT, LOOKS LEFT AND THEN RIGHT, SEEMS WIRED.

HE ADDRESSES US:

JIMMY (wired):

Sorry. I've been staying alert since earlier today. Bit stressful actually to be honest – think my cat's picked up on it, haven't seen him for a few hours. The hardest bit is not knowing what to be alert *for*. I have heard that they've found a dye that colours the Corona, so you can see it and avoid it… bit like a fart, but like a fart you can see, if you know what I mean. So it could be that. I did notice No. 28 go out earlier, come back with a Vienetta in her bag… is that essential? Am I supposed to alert someone? 'cause they don't tell yer, do they.

JIMMY RUBS HIS FACE, AGITATED…

That speech man! Aw, the speech! I couldn't stop being alert could I… 'cause there he is waffling on with all that bollocks, scripted, and all I can hear is

(in Boris's voice)

"We cannot… I repeat, we cannot… allow the rich to become less rich."

(reverts to own voice)

And then he goes on about some colour chart with panic levels – he lost me there, even though I was hyper alert – I was on it bigtime (top level).

He's a slippery character man; he is skilled in the dark arts of bullshit.

So basically… Red Alert – stay in and pray. Green Alert – biggest party on Earth, and he says we're somewhere Orange, which is either Might Die, Picnic, or half marathon.

JIMMY SWIGS SOME COFFEE – GOTTA STAY ALERT

To be fair, he did say he's gonna shine the light of science on it, so that's a relief – harder to find in the dark I expect. Sorry, sarcasm's just my way to deal with it, you know. I mean, it makes my piss boil that they don't tell you what to tell people like my old man – still locked in, still lonely, still living with his life dictated by idiots and selfish pricks. He's got a TV – he's seen the packed-out parks and the beaches and people not distancing. He sees the *real* attitude towards the old or the ill, as soon as they get in the way of sunbathing, or getting pissed, or big money. He's a number on a spreadsheet, right? Not a father, not a brother, or a grandad. He's expendable. High risk, low priority. Not worthless, but worth *less.*

And he's… … …alert.

END

LOVE BUGGED
BY
DAVID VINEY

A 10-minute play written to examine the need to release energy and tension in lockdown.

How long can you stay in ... before you freak out?

Starring Anna Jobarteh
Music written and performed by Jace Campbell
Directed by Michelle Parker
Produced by Paul Ludden / Mancmade Productions
Executive Producer Matt Bloom
Released 23rd October 2020
youtu.be/t2MTPR_yLAw

SCENE: INT. SINEAD'S FLAT. DAY.

LIGHTS UP

SINEAD (MID TO LATE 20'S, FULL MAKE-UP, GLAM TOP, BUT JOGGING BOTTOMS AND TRAINERS) IS HAVING A FACETIME PARTY WITH A FRIEND; EARPHONES IN, GLASS OF WINE IN ONE HAND, iPAD IN THE OTHER.

SHE DANCES IN FRONT OF A 2-SEATER SOFA WITH A MAGAZINE ON IT. NEXT TO THE SOFA IS A COFFEE TABLE WITH HER MOBILE PHONE.

SINEAD (singing Whitney Houston's 'How Will I Know' *badly*): *How will I know... How will I know... How will I know if he really loves me? I say a prayer with every...* Ah No! Come on, we can make this the last one. Ah, *pleeease!* You said you were a slave to the rhythm... ... ...well tell him you're *my* wife now. We... ... ...alright fine, but you owe me a Whitney and that is happening whether Dance-killer Darren likes it or not... Oh, hi Darren!... ...yeah, you too, can you put Kelly back...

SINEAD REALISES DARREN HAS DISCONNECTED FROM FACETIME.

SHE TAKES OUT HER EARPHONES, PUTS THEM AND THE iPAD ON THE TABLE.

SHE SITS DOWN, PUTS THE GLASS OF WINE ON THE FLOOR, REMOVES HER GLAM TOP TO REVEAL A CASUAL T-SHIRT UNDERNEATH AND DRAPES THE TOP OVER THE BACK OF THE SOFA.

SHE ADDRESSES THE AUDIENCE.

(mischievous) Video chat's like standing at a stable door; no one sees the bottom half. Just think yourself lucky I'm wearing pants.

SINEAD PICKS UP THE GOSSIP MAGAZINE AND BEGINS TO FLICK THROUGH ITS PAGES.

AFTER A FEW MOMENTS SHE LOWERS THE MAGAZINE...

3-month-old gossip. That I've read four times already. Celebrity gossip isn't really a thing right now – no one's falling out of clubs at 3am with their dance partner from *Strictly* – it's strictly lockdown mate. Strictly tension and telly, sitting in 3-day underwear wondering how long you can stay *in* before you freak *out*. Yeah... strictly torment on toast.

Neighbourly gossip's loud and proud though – people shout their business over their garden fences and backyards now; air their dirty laundry while they're hanging out the clean stuff:

(shouting) "Oh, hiya Vickie – love that top – the blue one...

(normal volume) Bet you wear that out on your four walks a day, don't you...

(shouting) Sorry, I was just saying – bet you can't wait to wear that Out Out...

(normal volume) Although it'll probably be worn out by then, after walking for hours like you do... breathing like you do... coughing like you do, you selfish ..."

SINEAD CUTS HERSELF OFF, PUTS DOWN THE MAGAZINE, SITS FORWARD.

Vickie is lovely, an absolute babe. What you witnessed there is what I'm calling 'Fever Diva' – not sure what the male equivalent is – possibly Covidiot-19, I don't know. But basically it's when my fears about being trapped indoors make me a stone cold bitch. We're allowed one hour of outdoor exercise a day and I regularly spend mine furious at anyone who might be flouting the rules – families with family members who don't look enough like each other – I mean, seriously did you adopt that kid or what? He looks nothing like you! Three of you have got black hair. His is dark brown at best. Send in the SWAT-team! Go, go, go! Honestly, I'm like the Paranoia Police – two teenagers walking down the street together – are you related? If YES, then you should really stop kissing, *eurgh!* If NO, please punch each other in the face, because I don't want to touch you, then go home. Separately.

Two joggers, who for some reason look like they wouldn't be housemates – do you live in the same house? If YES, go about your business. If NO, please accept my apologies for tasering you and locking you in a basement with all the other people I'm scared of, until this is over. Like I say... Fever Diva (apologetic) stone cold bitch. Paranoid Pandemic'er – real word.

SINEAD GRABS A HANDFUL OF HER T-SHIRT AND SMELLS IT... THEN HER ARMPITS...

(to self) Can't be... I washed my top half.

SINEAD LEANS FORWARD CONSPIRATORIALLY...

There was a party next door last night. Obviously I'm furious... that I wasn't invited. Oh don't look at me like that, I wouldn't have gone! Just would have been nice to RSVP wouldn't it... *I respectfully decline your invitation to spread the virus to friends and family, yours sincerely appalled, Sinead, kiss kiss.*

Never really got started anyway – dozy cow ordered a finger food buffet and a stripper online – ended up with a police Cease and Desist. And the copper's number. Or so she says. Can't trust a thing that comes out of her face that one.

SINEAD STANDS, WALKS OVER TO THE TABLE, PICKS UP HER PHONE, CHECKS IT WHILE TALKING TO US...

I can't work out if social media is keeping me sane, or driving me mad. Feels like I'm peeking through my fingers half the time, afraid of all the what-ifs. There's not enough *good* what-ifs. I mean what if that meme that's telling me something is fake news, is actually the fake news and the thing it said was fake is actually the true news? And what if it's two fake news hiding one big fake news?! Do you know what I mean? No, me neither.

SINEAD RETURNS TO HER SEAT ON THE SOFA.
SHE IS STILL SCROLLING...

Kelly put up a 'Wine-o'clock' status yesterday. I told her *What's the point – wine happens whenever now. And what's a clock?*

SINEAD PICKS UP THE WINE GLASS, 'CHEERS' THE AUDIENCE AND TAKES A GULP OF WINE.
SHE GETS A TEXT.

Ooh, text! Pays to be popular people...

SINEAD PUTS DOWN THE GLASS OF WINE AND READS THE TEXT.

(disappointed) I wish they'd extend the social distancing rules to messaging – if I had a pound for all the exes that have crawled out of the woodwork over the past month... well, I'd have two pounds. Maybe two pound fifty if I count Jason. Got short-changed there – should've listened to the alarm bells when he said I reminded him of his mum.

SINEAD LOOKS LIKE SHE CAN TASTE THE BITTER MEMORY.
SHE PUTS HER PHONE DOWN ON THE SOFA.

I'm not alone. I don't mean alone as in lockdown – everyone's in lockdown. I mean in this flat. Damian's out exercising. We had a row – technically Part 2 of an argument we had yesterday. So now we're exercising at different times. It'll blow over obviously – he's my *Manimal* – real word. But if he keeps chewing like an *actual* animal, I swear to God I'm gonna kill him! Crime of passion. No court in the land would send me down for it either – my defence lawyer would do a reconstruction in the courtroom, where an actor (who looks just like the annoying get) would eat Nachos, or nuts, or yoghurt, or anything DEAD LOUD! And I guarantee that Jury would be unanimous – Not Guilty.

It was fine when either of us could walk away. Now storming off has a one in three chance of bumping into each other – living room, bathroom, bedroom. I suppose one of us could get in the loft, but that's a bit much innit.

Don't get me wrong – when he's good, he's almost great. It's just, we're not used to spending this much time together… I'm noticing a few 'quirks'… like he's got this thing where he scratches his nose when we're watching TV and it's right…

SINEAD PUTS HER HAND BY HER FACE TO ILLUSTRATE PERIPHERAL VISION.

…I can't even talk about it, it's making me mad.

But I love him.

He can be a right pain in the arse, but he's my pain in the arse and he's sweet in a non-clingy, non-cheesy kind of way and he cooks, he cleans – he's basically a 1950's housewife. I'm like Gas-Mark-What-You-On-About-Mate, so right now without him it'd be discount Easter Eggs for breakfast, lunch and tea…

SINEAD PONDERS A DIET OF EASTER EGGS.

...Ok, so that's a bad example. But I am so messy! He puts up with his fair share from me. If I drop something, I *will* do an assessment and if I can live without it, it's staying where it is.

And I stop films half way through when I'm bored.

But he does leave his toe-nail clippings on the table...

SINEAD LOOKS AT THE TABLE IN DISGUST.

...so swings and roundabouts I suppose.

Gran says if she can manage 36 years without murdering Grandad, I can manage three months of lockdown. I hope we make it to 36 years. I hope we make it to 36 *months*.

He's 'forgotten' his key as well. He thinks I'm daft, but I know exactly what he's up to... he thinks that if I open that door for him and he pulls some stupid face (well, more stupid than it is already), I'll laugh and he'll have a tactical advantage. Never gonna happen mate – I've been practising my disappointment face for years. Go on, give me the funniest face you've got...

SINEAD PUTS ON HER BEST DISAPPOINTMENT FACE, THEN AFTER A MOMENT...

...See! No flinching. No contest. Boom!

WE HEAR A KNOCK AT THE DOOR.

That's him now.

Listen, whatever you do don't tell him I said he was sweet – I'll never hear the end of it.

SINEAD EXITS STAGE LEFT TO ANSWER DOOR.

SINEAD (back stage, laughing loudly): Whatever, stop smiling you muppet. This doesn't mean you've won.

LIGHTS OUT

END

There are

17 Fucks

4 bullshits

2 Arseholes

5 Shits 1 Shite

1 gobshite

1 Prick

1 Asshole

and a Codshit

in this book

All of which are integral to the plot

** while stocks last*